MORRIE
IN HIS OWN
WORDS

MORRIE
IN HIS OWN
WORDS

Morrie Schwartz

Introduction by Paul Solman

WALKER AND COMPANY

NEW YORK

First published in the United States of America in 1996 by Walker Publishing Company, Inc.; new hardcover edition published in 1999.

Published simultaneously in Canada by Fitzhenry and Whiteside, Markham, Ontario L3R 4T8

Library of Congress Cataloging-in-Publication Data
Schwartz, Morris S.
[Letting go]
Morrie: in his own words/Morrie Schwartz;
introduction by Paul Solman.
p.   cm.
Originally published: Letting go/Morrie Schwartz. New York:
Walker and Co., 1996.
ISBN 0-8027-1355-6 (hc.)
1. Schwartz, Morris S.—Health.   2. Amyotrophic lateral sclerosis—Patients—United States—Biography.   3. Terminally ill—Psychology.
4. Adjustment (Psychology)   I. Title.
RC406.A24S39   1999
362.1'9683—dc21
[B]   98-56448
CIP

Book design by Mary Jane DiMassi

Printed in the United States of America

8   10   9   7

CONTENTS

INTRODUCTION

Paul Solman

His name: Morris Schwartz. "But call me Morrie," he insisted, even to Ted Koppel, who obliged on three *Nightline* specials in 1995, half-hour interviews which helped make this wise old man a national icon.

Morrie's reason for appearing on network television was as straightforward as the man himself: At age seventy-eight, more fully alive than ever, Morrie was dying—of a degenerative disease known as amyotrophic lateral sclerosis (ALS), or Lou Gehrig's disease. And though actually a rather humble guy, Morrie realized he could use the media for one final accomplishment in an achievement-filled life: to flush death out of the closet, to help people talk openly about illness, decay, and the end we all share.

"Learn how to live," Morrie wrote, "and you'll know how to die; learn how to die, and you'll know how to live." Morrie's message was not only for the sick and those close to them, but for the healthy as well. His was a way of looking at the world, a point of view he expressed on *Nightline,* in the *Boston Globe,* and on radio and television nationwide.

And people responded, powerfully. Morrie struck a nerve. Hundreds of viewers, listeners, and readers wrote to him—for advice, for comfort, but most of all to thank him for giving a voice to issues they have been struggling with in silence.

After all, here was a man with a disease that destroys, without exception, the ability of nerves to signal muscles. The muscles stop working and atrophy, in Morrie's case starting with the legs. Then you die.

But Morrie's response to the death sentence was to create a sort of living memorial service. A joyous one. He watched Marx Brothers movies, steeped himself in all the humor he could find. He let friends know he wanted them to visit. And he began writing the aphorisms which form the core of this book.

The book is, in a sense, Morrie's last will and testament—of how to live passionately and calmly, right to the end. As he lost muscle function he handwrote the aphorisms ever more slowly and unsteadily, but with surer and surer conviction. He thought at first they could stand on their own without elaboration. But he came to realize that most readers need help putting them into practice. The aphorisms are written in a sort of how-to shorthand: They're mantras that, by themselves, can seem as formidable as they are profound.

"Grieve and mourn for yourself not once or twice, but again and again," Morrie writes.

But how? We're not all Morries. Most of us don't know why we should grieve and mourn, don't know how.

And so Morrie began to dictate the biographical commentaries that accompany the aphorisms—trying to help teach readers how he'd arrived at the aphorisms, how he meant for people to understand them, and most of all, how to help readers apply the aphorisms and internalize them.

The taping took place over the course of several months and sometimes the effort was enormous. By the end, struggling to cough to bring up phlegm, Morrie could only watch as the microphone slipped off his chest and wait for it to be propped back up. But the more we taped, the more apparent it became that not only were the aphorisms workable, they were part of something much larger. Morrie had a consistent worldview, one that had been evolving for most of his life and that he was only now articulating as a whole. To paraphrase it may sound hokey to some, reassuringly familiar to others. But regardless, to Morrie, life was a process of opening oneself lovingly—to other people, to the world, ultimately, to something larger than ourselves. To the last instant, Morrie was full of wonder and joy. The way he lived his final year was this great teacher's final lesson.

The aphorisms flow from his worldview; the worldview, in turn, from Morrie's biography. And so it helps to know something about him before taking on the text.

A short, freckle-faced redhead, born in Chicago of Russian Jewish immigrants and brought up in the New York ghetto, Morrie "dressed like a schlepper, with half-pants that came to my knees," as he described himself in one of his last interviews. He was, he remembered, "always kind of cheerful, but sad inside." That's because his mother died when he was eight, forcing her son to withdraw into himself.

"I had become aware of vulnerability," he said, "that something precious could be snatched away at any moment."

Growing up motherless sensitized Morrie to loss and his need for other people. A nurturing stepmother who adored both Morrie and his younger brother instilled a compassion for others, combined with a passion for learning.

Morrie made it to New York's tuition-free City College. Turned down for military service in World War II because of a punctured eardrum, he decided to apply to graduate school. He was torn between sociology and psychology.

"I'd always been interested in psychology,"

Morrie said. "What tipped the scales was that psychology involved working with rats." He wound up studying sociology at the University of Chicago.

Reading the likes of Carl Rogers, Harry Stack Sullivan, and Martin Buber, Morrie responded to their philosophy: open yourself up to what you're really feeling. The emphasis wasn't solely on the individual, as psychology would have it, or strictly on society, as the word "sociology" suggests. Instead, Morrie was drawn to the connection between the two: an emerging field known as social psychology.

With Morrie's first job came his first epiphany, because in order to work on a research project at a mental hospital, he had to undergo psychoanalysis.

"I started to understand the full impact of my mother's death . . . and mourn my loss," he said in his last interview. Morrie described therapy as "cathartic"; it was his first experience with seeing himself at a distance, becoming a witness to himself. As the aphorisms make clear, this became a key technique for coping with his death.

In collaboration with Alfred H. Stanton, Morrie began working on a ward in a nontraditional psychoanalytic mental hospital, watching the troubled and tormented, observing the staff and their relationships with patients. What struck him was the huge influence the attitudes of those around them had on the patients. Morrie was there to observe and talk with everyone—even those patients crouching alone in the corners. He related to them civilly, humbly. He opened his heart as best he could. Gradually, he got them to respond. The importance of opening oneself to others, no matter who they are, and the impact of community on the individual became clear to him.

The book that resulted from the research, "The Mental Hospital" by Stanton and Schwartz, became a classic of social psychology, influencing an entire generation of practitioners. Not long after the book's publication, Morrie was offered a faculty position at Brandeis. For almost four decades, to a year before his death, he continued to be a participant-observer. His undergraduate course on "group process" was an annual laboratory in learning to be nonjudgmental, to see yourself as a part of a community and open yourself to it. In short, Morrie spent the rest of his life practicing what he had begun to preach.

He had help. To his wife and two sons, he attributed his ability to suppress his ego, to understand that others can be even more important to you than you yourself are.

To "Greenhouse," a low-fee psychotherapy organization and community he formed with friends and colleagues in the '60s, he ascribed his ability to mourn loss, starting with his mother and ending with himself.

To his colleagues in the then-radical Brandeis sociology department, he credited his continuing championing of the underdog, his politics of inclusion and equality.

Morrie even thanked asthma, a disease which afflicted him relatively late in life and, he said, taught him how to distance himself from the panic of dying (or seeming to), as he gasped for breath.

In his late sixties, Morrie embarked on his final stretch of road. He learned to meditate. To Morrie, it was an extension of the practice of psychotherapy—of getting distance on himself, of learning how to live in the moment, of opening up to the universe at large. It was, in one sense, the beginning of Morrie's "spiritual practice," as that phrase is typically employed. In another sense, it was the culmination of a spiritual practice Morrie had begun decades before.

It is from Morrie's journey that the aphorisms come, the aphorisms around which this book is built. From Aesop to Jesus to haiku to Nietzsche, the concise insight has had an honored place in world culture. In the age of television and "bits" of information, people sometimes mock brief utterances as "sound bites." Morrie wouldn't have worried about that. He considered these messages sound bites for the soul. All souls.

Morrie died peacefully at his home on November 4, 1995.

Paul Solman was a student of Morrie Schwartz's at Brandeis.

PART I

*Understanding Where
You Are Now*

LIVING WITH PHYSICAL LIMITATIONS

Whenever a lessening of a physical power occurs, it will always feel too soon. Expect this reaction. Perhaps by preparing for it mentally, you can soften its impact.

When I learned I had ALS in 1994, I said to myself, "Am I going to die, or am I going to live?" By that I meant, am I going to withdraw, as many people probably do, and give up on the world because it's been so horrible to me now, or am I going to live? I decided I was going to live. But could I live the way I wanted to live, with dignity, with courage, with humor, with relatedness? I wasn't sure whether I could do it or not, but I said, "I'm going to try my best." I made a willful determination to call on my resources to enable me to live with composure, as I put it, and so far I've been able to do so.

Since then I have watched many of my physical functions deteriorate as the nerves in my body gradually starve off my muscles. It is getting more and more difficult for me to feed myself. When I shave in the morning and when I eat, I find I cannot lift my hand all the way. It's as if I have a big weight on my hands.

My swallowing is more difficult now. I cough a lot. Sometimes I have to chew my food very, very finely to get it down, and I don't know how much longer I'll be able to get enough nourishment without needing a feeding tube. It was difficult when I had to adjust to no longer being able to walk, but impaired swallowing is the first really major loss for me. The second is my speech. When I make the "o" sound, it gets caught in my throat. And my speech has become somewhat slurred. That's one of the beginning signs that I'm losing my voice.

All my life I have expected to talk. That expectation is so ingrained in me that when I have to face not talking, it's a tremendous shock. So now I'm saying to myself, What will it be like when I cannot articulate—when I can't give a command or ask for something, or say something that is in my heart or in my head? I don't know what it'll be like. But I'll try to find a way to take advantage of silence, because maybe that's the way to really hear yourself.

It's going to be an interesting challenge. I'm already saying to family and friends, "You'll tell me what you're thinking and feeling, and you'll feel my response. I won't be able to articulate it, but you'll see it in my face." My face, I think, will still be very mobile and should remain expressive. But if they want to discuss something and get my feedback or help, they will have to frame much of what they are saying as questions that I can answer in a yes-or-no code. That's the way I am approaching the coming loss of my speech. I hope I'll discover new means and mechanisms when the time arrives.

I don't think you can be totally prepared for diminished capacities by anticipating them—there is nothing as powerful as experiencing these losses. You can think about what might happen, and what you would like to do and so on, but until the time actually arrives, you don't have the experience. And that's what makes the difference as to what I will do and how I'll do it. I undoubtedly will get depressed for a while. How long a while, I don't know, but that's my normal reaction. And then, maybe two days or three days later, I'll start to bounce back.

Whatever powers you feel yourself losing, be it walking or talking or being as mentally sharp as before, the more you can anticipate their impact, the easier your adjustment will be.

Accept yourself, your physical condition, and your fate as they are at the present moment.

❧

Recently I read a useful book entitled *Betrayal of the Body* by Alexander Lowen, M.D. His idea is that we think our body should be perfect or at least should be functioning at a high level all the time. When it does not, we feel betrayed by it as if there's some ordained commandment that we always will be healthy and our body always will be responsive. I suspect this is a way of convincing ourselves of our immortality. We have not quite accepted the idea that we're mortal, that we're vulnerable, that we, indeed, at any moment can be laid low.

Expect that it's going to be harder and take longer to do things. Be prepared to do things in ways that are very different from the ways you did them before.

❧❧❧

When I started to lose strength in my legs, I was unprepared for how severe the weakness was becoming until I landed on the ground. I was with my brother, and he had pulled the car up right to the curb of the building I was going to enter for an acupuncture treatment. I got out of the car as if I were steady on my feet, which I was not. I had a cane with me, but at that point I couldn't use it effectively. Before I knew it, I was lying on the ground.

Restriction on my mobility has taught me that I have to inhibit my impulses. I am a very impulsive guy—not so much psychologically as behaviorally. I see something, I want to go for it. Now I have to inhibit my impulses and redefine what's possible for me and what's not. It's a great lesson for me because all my life I've been very agile, very quick, and, I'd say, very supple, really going after the physical things I wanted. I can't do this anymore. All the way down the line—from getting into and out of my bed to sitting on the john—I have to be transported everywhere.

It has been very hard to adjust to the loss of mobility, the loss of freedom. But it also has been a terrific challenge, learning to inhibit my impulses. That's the kind of mental flexibility you need to adopt—the capacity to see and choose alternative ways of doing things.

Get as much help as you can when you need it.

❧❧❧

A couple of years ago a friend of mine who was about eighty-five was getting ready to cross the street on a wet, rainy day. A young person offered to help him across. My friend refused the help and was hit by a car, an accident which eventually brought about his death. Despite his age, he was still trying to assert his independence and not allow himself to say, "Yes, I need the help of this person."

People refuse help because they feel their self-esteem depends on their being "independent." We fear that somehow or other we have been diminished because we need, want, and desire another person's help. That's because of our independent, individualistic culture. We have a sense that we should be like the mythical cowboy. Free, easy, able to do anything, able to take on and conquer anything and live in the world without the need for other people. The Lone Ranger type.

That's an image a lot of men, especially, carry around. They don't allow themselves to develop a sense of their interpersonal needs. I think it's very unfortunate. For we need each other more than we know.

In fact, these needs are very great on the emotional, psychological level, as well as on the physical level. But we tend to avoid exposing these needs like the plague. From my point of view, it makes so much more sense to be clear about your needs and realize that you need others, just as they need you.

The manner of the person offering help can have a positive or negative impact on what the response will be. Here are some suggestions if you are visiting or caring for someone who needs assistance.

First, don't offer to do something if you really don't want to do it, because your family member or loved one is likely to sense your feelings and will find it harder to accept your help without feeling angry or humiliated. If you are asked to do something that is too inconvenient or uncomfortable for you, be honest about your reasons for declining—if possible, help set up an alternative way for the task to be done by someone else.

Try not to treat your loved one with kid gloves. Be specific when asking him if he needs help. If you see he is having difficulty getting a drinking straw out of its wrapper, offer to open the wrapper for him without making a big deal of it. Be matter-of-fact in your manner when appropriate.

Be respectful and maintain the usual boundaries of propriety when possible. For example, don't lift your friend's head and start fluffing her pillow without asking. Regardless of how incapacitated she is, she will want to know that you still respect her autonomy.

Don't stay preoccupied with your body or your illness. Recognize that your body is not your total self, only part of it.

🌿

When you're seriously ill (and I speak from experience), it's so easy to become preoccupied with your body and its illness. I used to run therapy groups, and in one group there was a man who had an illness that he would never specify to the group. But every time the group met he would just complain about the illness and how debilitating and difficult it was—how impossible it was for him. He went on and on. Not only did he contribute to his own misery by berating himself over his illness, but he was agitating everybody else in the group. Finally, they rejected him.

I know it's not easy to focus on something else when *your* body aches. But it's important to try. Preoccupation with your ailment makes you a prisoner of your body because the body is then dictating your whole life; in turn, your whole life starts to revolve around injury or dysfunction or deficiency. There are healthier and more pleasing ways to spend your efforts and energy.

When we have an injury to the body, we tend to think it's an injury to the self. But it was very important for me to make clear to myself that my body is only part of who I am. We are much greater than the sum of our physical parts. The way we look at the world is fashioned by our values and our thoughts about good and evil, things that go into making us who we are. We have emotions, insights, and intuitions.

My contention is that as long as you have other faculties—the emotional, psychological, intuitive faculties—you haven't lost yourself or even diminished yourself. Don't be ashamed when you're physically limited or dysfunctional; don't think that you're any less because of your condition. In fact, I feel I am even more myself than I was before I got this illness because I have been able to transcend many of the psychological and emotional limitations I had before I developed ALS.

2

HANDLING FRUSTRATION

*Expect things to be inaccessible,
unattainable, unreachable. When they are,
don't get too frustrated or angry. If you do,
let it be short-lived.*

Simply speaking, frustration is the result of an impulse being inhibited or an impulse being acted on where the objective has not been achieved successfully. For example, I want a pencil because I want to write a short note about something, but the pencil is a distance away from me. I want to have the pencil, but since I cannot move my body enough to be able to reach it, I don't try. My frustration comes not from the fact that I can't reach it but from being inhibited from acting on my impulse.

If the pencil were near enough that I could almost reach it, I would try for it . . . and if it remained out of my grasp, I would be frustrated because my efforts had failed. Either way, my frustration is compounded by the fact that without the pencil, I can't write what I wanted to write. Instead of becoming more agitated over my diminished mobility, I nip my frustration in the bud by asking someone to come into the room and hand me a pencil.

Physical frustrations are bad enough, but I'll bet there isn't anyone reading this book (regardless of age or state of health) who hasn't been stymied by an inability to remember a word or a name that he or she knows.

For me, it goes like this: I'm in the middle of a sentence, and I need just the right word. I can't think of it. I get very frustrated. But—and here's the point—if I wait and don't struggle to force it to the surface, the word usually comes. I've been through this often enough to know that I will remember it eventually, but I want to think of it now.

That's a basic characteristic of frustration. I want what I want when I want it: When I don't get it, I'm frustrated. But if I don't demand that it be there at this very moment, the frustration is reduced and the objective still will be achieved, though it takes a while.

Expect stressful situations to occur as your illness progresses or acts up. Develop an approach to managing your emotions during these occurrences.

⚘

Asking for help when you need it is one of the best ways to keep from becoming overly frustrated when your illness flares up. Patience is another, so when I can't find the word I want, I tell myself to wait until it comes to me. You have to develop an alternative kind of response to whatever is upsetting you.

Suppose I really want a glass of water and there's no one around to get it for me. My arms are too weak for me to wheel myself into the kitchen or the bathroom and get the water for myself. What's the alternative? Well, I have to give up wanting the water. I reconcile myself to doing without it. Sometimes that's very hard to do. Sometimes it's not so hard. But if you don't learn to manage these frustrations, they will build up and you'll find yourself living in a constant state of agitation. For your own sake, don't make your life any more difficult than it has to be.

Watch for emotional, spiritual, or behavioral regressions when you are most vulnerable. Try to avoid, minimize, or stop your regression.

❧❧❧

Frustration arises easily when you are in a physically or emotionally vulnerable state, especially when you are tired, sleepless, or anxious. At those times, it is tempting to let yourself regress and have a temper tantrum when you don't get what you want. But you're not a baby, and you owe it to yourself and to those around you to try to maintain your composure even when you are feeling exhausted or worried or insecure.

That does not mean you should keep your feelings bottled up. Quite the contrary, you need to express yourself on a regular basis. But be aware of how your present state of mind in-

fluences the way you respond to people and situations. If you are nervously awaiting test
results, you may be short-tempered when a
meal arrives late or if a friend calls to cancel a
visit. When you are under unusual stress, moni-
tor what you say more carefully than usual so
you don't take out your frustrations on others.
If you do respond in a way that you know is
inappropriate or hurtful, go ahead and apologize.

Be honest with those who are close to you.
Let them know that you are in a bad mood and,
if possible, be specific about the nature of what
has you out of sorts. Who knows—if you tell
them you are tired because you did not sleep
well, they may offer to give you a relaxing mas-
sage or read something soothing to you. If you
are anxious because of a change in your condition, talk about your feelings to a family member or friend. And if you are the person who is
listening, don't feel that your loved one is look-

ing to you for answers or solutions. Often the fact that you listened sympathetically will make him feel better.

When you are utterly frustrated or angry, express these feelings. You don't have to be nice all the time—just most of the time.

❧

When you are frustrated and angry, you shouldn't be afraid to vent your anger, though not necessarily toward someone else. You can curse silently under your breath or even out loud if the situation permits. Venting your feelings is not inconsistent with maintaining your composure. In fact, expressing negative feelings periodically helps alleviate frustration in the long run. It is healthy to complain, show anger, or cry sometimes. When I express my anger out loud to people who will understand, it is great to have someone who will listen and hear my complaining for what it is, without telling me, "Oh, don't say that," or "You're more mature than that."

When I'm angry and complaining, I want to be angry and complaining. I find that complaining and being open about my frustration is cathartic, and I know my mood is not going to last very long. Pretty soon I will be back to my usual self. That's a whole lot better than censoring my feelings and letting them eat away at me.

If you don't have someone who will listen to your complaints without becoming upset or judgmental, write about your anger or dictate into a tape recorder. You can gain distance and perspective by writing down what you are going through. When I write about my experiences, they seem to take a place outside of me on the paper. When I'm reading about them, it is as if the events were happening to someone else, and I can look at that "someone else" more objectively.

Humor, too, can be a useful way to defuse frustration. It also helps you to be more objective about your situation. Stand back and laugh at yourself whenever you can. Let's say you've dropped your book for the fifth time this morning and this time it landed faceup, open to the page you had been reading. Try to see the humor in the concept of "long-distance" reading rather than let yourself focus on how frustrating it is to have diminished coordination. Laughing is good for you, but avoid using humor to put yourself down.

Some people who are under considerable stress from illness are afraid to show anger or frustration because they fear that their complaints might snowball. But I say, "Wherever the feeling goes, let it go." If a lot of frustrations have been building up, you need to talk about them. If talking causes your feelings to escalate and you start complaining about other things, recognize that that's what you're doing and accept it. Have confidence in yourself and realize that eventually you will be better off because you have expressed your feelings.

The morning I was dictating this chapter I was full of complaints. My legs were hurting. My breathing was more labored. My swallowing was more difficult. I was getting indigestion while I was eating. I was having trouble with my bowels. And on and on. But after I groused about everything, I started to feel better. I don't think I would have felt just as well if I hadn't gotten it all out. I'm a great believer in complaining—and my complaints have never snowballed to the extent that I could not get over them.

Everyone has to find his or her own way of handling these things. My way may be helpful to you, but if it's better for you to cut off your complaints at a certain point, then do so, or don't start complaining in the first place. But whatever your way of responding, you have to test it out. Is it really better to hold yourself back, or are you inhibiting yourself because you're worried about what the other person will think? There's no fixed formula. It's a matter of being aware and focusing on yourself and learning how you best take care of yourself around these issues.

One of my biggest frustrations occurred a few years before I developed ALS, and in some ways it turned out to be a proving ground that helped prepare me for this stage of my life.

You probably never would guess it to look at me, but I used to love to dance. I have been dancing since I was twelve years old. In 1928, my father, stepmother, brother, and I lived in a three-room apartment in the Bronx that had a big kitchen where my family spent most of our time. Whenever I heard music on the radio, I would grab a broomstick for my partner and start dancing around the kitchen.

Music lessons were out of the question because of the expense, and since I couldn't sing, dancing was my only form of musical expression. I used to love watching Fred Astaire dance with Ginger Rogers and all his other partners in the movies; that fantasy world was a wonderful escape from my impoverished real life.

After I grew up, I danced through my sixties, going to a place called Dance Free. There was an admission fee, but once you were inside, you could dance as much as you liked without charge. I was usually the oldest person there. I would have a towel around my neck, because I sweated so much and I danced up a storm. I remember telling a friend that if I ever stopped dancing, I would die.

But in 1984 I had to give up dancing because I developed severe asthma.

Thus, asthma precipitated my first real crisis about my body. I was sixty-seven years old and had never been ill before. Suddenly, there were nights I stood by the window gasping for breath, not knowing whether the next breath would come. That's how bad my asthma was until it was brought under control with steroids. To deal with my anxiety, I went for a few months to see a psychiatrist, who really helped me take my illness more in stride.

Learning to come to terms with the panic of asthma attacks made me more familiar with the tension of being ill. ALS is more serious than asthma, but I am less frightened by my present condition because of my asthma experiences.

When I hear music I used to dance to, I still have the desire to get up and soar. It is frustrating to know that the muscles in my extremities are so weak I can't even tap my foot or my finger. But I am happy to report that even though I can't dance, I still enjoy listening to dance music.

3

GRIEVING FOR YOUR LOSSES

Grieve and mourn for yourself, not once or twice, but again and again. Grieving is a great catharsis and comfort and a way of keeping yourself composed.

rieving, mourning, crying are natural emotions. They come easily and readily if they're not subverted by cultural prohibitions, expectations, and distortions. Grieving is an important part of living because experiencing loss is inevitable for everyone. The older you become, the more losses you sustain. Therefore, you need to work out a way of handling grief.

The best way is to let yourself grieve freely and mourn losses. You may want to cry about them. Without this kind of release you're apt to be left with an inner pain that can affect your life in many ways.

We ordinarily think of mourning for others—our parents and our other loved ones—but we don't think very much about mourning for ourselves. Mourning for myself has made an important contribution to my composure. How do I do it? I let myself experience the grief, the sadness, the despair, the bitterness, the anger, the dread, the regret, and the sense of finishing before my time. I let the tears flow until they dry up. And then I start to think about what I'm crying about. I'm crying about my own death, my departure from people I love, the sense of unfinished business and of leaving this beautiful world. Crying has helped me gradually come to accept the end—the fact that all living things die.

Grieving never ends with one outpouring. The need to cry, to mourn, to groan, to sob may come back time and time again. Let yourself feel the depth of your tears, your sense of loss, the pain, and the emptiness that you feel because of it. Don't be afraid to come back to it as many times as you need to. In my case I cry a lot. Small tears and large tears and minitears. I cry alone. I cry with other people.

I see mourning as a way of paying respect to life. It's how we humans pay respect to our dead, to the people who have departed, to our losses. In the Jewish tradition, we mourn a loved one by tearing our clothing (symbolically, tearing our hearts) to express our sadness and our sense of loss.

You can express a sense of loss in other ways. But I knew that crying would work for me because of an experience I had had in a therapy workshop years ago.

The leader had people enact scenes that

were important in their lives. Finally, I said, "I want to do my scene. I want to do my mother's death."

The leader said, "Okay, I'll set up the scene." He put people in different roles: my grandmother, grandfather, and father. And he dressed up a box as a casket and pointed to it and said, "That's your mother. What do you want to say to her?"

I was overwhelmed with emotion. I just screamed out, "Why did you leave me?" And then I broke down completely.

I was in my midfifties when this happened. My mother had died nearly half a century earlier, but I cried for hours. I'd stop and start over again. It was the longest I'd ever cried. And I felt that it was a powerful transitional experience. It changed my whole attitude toward dealing with my mother's death.

Now, as I cry for myself and mourn the future separation from the people I love, and the past separation from my mother, I am sometimes crying as well for the pain in the world—the cruelty, meanness, and murder. There are many things to mourn and grieve in addition to marking one's own losses and bereavements.

After I've cried for a while, I find comfort from expressing these deep feelings, comfort in knowing that I can express them—that they are there, that I can get them out. My feelings strengthen rather than weaken me.

After going through this kind of mourning, it's so much easier to face the day, so much easier to do the things I have to do with my family and friends, to be loving and ready for whatever happens.

✄ Tips on Healthy Grieving ✄

What's the difference between the kind of grieving that makes you feel weighed down and depressed and the kind that produces catharsis? Unresolved feelings of guilt can obscure the grieving process. If you have a lot of anger you don't want to recognize, or if there are issues you never really worked out fully with the person you're grieving, you are fixated on regrets, and the grieving may not be as "productive" as it would be if you were grieving mostly out of loss and love.

Should you weep alone? Is it okay to cry in front of others? People feel ashamed to be seen weeping. They say, "Oh, I shouldn't do this. I'm grown up. That's not proper behavior." Or they don't want somebody else to see them cry because it will make the other person sad. Or they fear people will think they are weak and inadequate.

It's true that it isn't easy to watch someone cry, especially someone you love. But my advice to friends and family is to encourage the person to grieve. The best way to respond to a person who is crying is to be sympathetic and empathic. Be encouraging by saying something like, "It's okay, I'll be here with you," or "I will be here for you to help you in whatever way you need until you stop crying. And if you want to stop and then continue, it's okay with me."

When you're grieving, you should not try to hide your grief from visitors and family and friends. Your attitude should be: "That's where I am and I'm accepting it. I'd like you to accept it, too. Don't falsify the reality. And if you want to cry along with me, fine. If you don't, that's also fine. But it shouldn't upset you because you should realize it's important for me to do this and it ultimately makes me feel much better than if I didn't do it. Therefore, you should take comfort in seeing that I am doing it."

The catharsis or relief you get doesn't mean your grief is all over and has been resolved or that crying has taken care of the situation. Rather, for the moment you come to some stasis, some sense of rest.

*Make an agreement with your family
and friends to remind you when you are
depressed, anxious, despairing, or lacking in
composure that you do not want to stay that
way. Ask them for a compassionate nudge.*

❧❧

This might seem to contradict my advice
that people should be encouraged to grieve, but
there is a difference between thwarting or sup-
pressing someone's emotional outlet and helping the person redirect his or her feelings.
Sometimes I sink into depression and it takes
over my emotions, just as ALS takes over my
body. It helps if I get a compassionate nudge
from someone who'll say, "Hey, Morrie, when
you were in good spirits you said that we should
remind you—but if that makes you feel worse,
I won't remind you. If it makes you feel better,

I'm reminding you." Make light of the somber mood in some way. That nudge could produce some distance that enables you to get hold of your inner turmoil and step back from your suffering.

Outside assistance may be more indirect. For example, if a friend sees that you are becoming depressed, he might try to distract you or give you something—like an embrace that he knows will lift your spirits a little bit. Or he might tell you you're really important to him or share a joke or a funny story with you. There are a lot of different things a friend or family member can do to help you out of a blue mood.

It's not a simple process to get out of depression. It depends on how deep it is, what it's about, how long in your life you've had it, how recurrent it's been, whether you have developed your own ways of getting out of it, and so on. Each case is different. Clinical depressions are very difficult to shake and may require professional intervention. My advice is aimed at what's called a reactive depression, when you are reacting to something that's happened in your life such as intense pain, loss, or a severing of something you held dear. When you are chronically or terminally ill, you undoubtedly will become depressed about your illness and need the support of family and friends to pull out of it.

After you have wept and grieved for your physical losses, cherish the functions and the life you have left.

Coming full circle is what grieving is about: to come to terms with the loss and to arrive at a point where you go back to your way of living and seeing life as worthwhile.

You're never finished with grieving if what you are mourning is something deep and important. As time goes by, I mourn less often and less deeply. But the goal should not be to avoid or stop grieving; the idea is to use grieving as a healthy outlet for your emotions.

It's important to recognize the difference between self-pity and grieving. I'm self-pitying if I say, "Why me? Why has God let this happen?" If I say, "This is a terrible thing that has happened to me. I feel awful about it," I am acknowledging my sadness.

Self-pity can be a beginning phase in the grieving process. But you have to move beyond recriminations in order to connect with your ordinary life, in all its sadness and joy. The next chapter will help you make that transition to acceptance.

Who knows why I got this illness, where it came from, and whether God has anything to do with it? Whereas if I accept that it's a reality and recognize the important things I'm losing, I can grieve for my lost functions and for the fact that I'm very far down the path toward death. I grieve about losing my loved ones. This is grief and mourning that represents the essence of life. Having paid my respects through grieving, I can stop brooding over the things I've been deprived of and feel grateful for what I have— people who help me and family and friends whose love I cherish.

 4

REACHING ACCEPTANCE

Try to develop an inner emotional or spiritual peace to balance the distresses of your body. You might begin by learning to accept "what is" for you at any particular time.

A cceptance is more difficult than it needs to be because people in our society basically refuse to accept our common fate—death. We are all going to die, but we tend to deny it or run away from it or feel, irrationally, that it won't happen to us. If you can accept the inevitability of your own death, it may be a little easier for you to confront serious or disabling illness.

Too often we have the sense that we should be able to change everything, that technology will take care of whatever goes wrong. Our credo is, "If it's not the way I want it, I'll find a way to fix it." That's fine for lots of situations. If you can change your condition for the better, do it. Acceptance becomes an issue if getting well is not an option for you.

Maybe we'll discover a cure for ALS twenty years from now, but we don't have one now, so I have to accept the fact that I have a disabling and fatal disease. A lot of experiments are going on, but if I'm expecting some great miracle cure in the next two weeks, it's going to be very hard for me to accept my situation. It's a matter of being quite realistic about seeing the truth clearly. Then you can determine whether your condition is changeable or not. If you discover that it's not changeable, either you accept it, or you're always going to be frustrated, always pushing against the grain to no avail.

Acceptance doesn't happen right away. My own experience is that I went in and out of acceptance. I would accept having ALS, then I'd get agitated about it for a while. I'd accept it again. Back and forth. After a while I came to a place where the disbelief and the unacceptance lessened and I was able to say, "Okay, that's the way it is." I don't know if one ever arrives at complete acceptance. I do know I have reached a comfortable level of acceptance. When we talk about acceptance, we have to think about the developmental aspect of it over time: Acceptance becomes stronger and stronger until finally it's all there.

Expect to feel like a dependent child and an independent adult at different times.

❧

The idea of every society is to move each person away from complete dependency to relative independence. That's what growing up is about. You develop trust in your parents, confidence that they will care for you and guide you so you will become sufficiently able to go on your independent path.

Serious illness may rob you of some of your independence, but don't confuse being dependent on others with being childish. The point is that most of us have enough independence and dependency to keep the two in proper balance. Balance is the aim, not total exclusion of either from your life.

Very early on in my illness, I recognized that I would have to accept my dependency. Otherwise this was not going to work. I went farther: I said, "I'm not just going to accept help, but I'm going to indulge it. I'm going to let myself feel the pleasure of being dependent." Since my mother became very sick when I was five or six,

I missed a lot of loving mothering when I was at a dependent stage, so I think part of me still yearns for nurturing. I allow myself to enjoy being cared for when people do things to help me.

At some point, be prepared to deal with profound contradictory feelings—for example, wanting to live and wanting to die, loving others and disliking them.

❧✦❧

I call this the tension of opposites, and I find that many of the feelings I'm involved with have two opposite sides. We have ambivalent feelings about many things. I don't think we're aware of some of the negative parts because they make us too uncomfortable. For example, most of us are more than willing to declare our deep love for someone, but it's harder to admit having a little

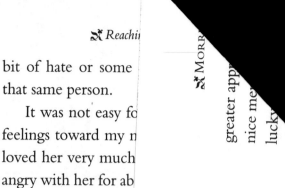

bit of hate or some
that same person.

It was not easy fo
feelings toward my n
loved her very much
angry with her for ab
it was not her fault s

I don't think anybody has a pure relationship with anyone else. There are always negative factors involved, and those negative factors stir up unpleasant feelings. Face them, or they can make you angry and bitter.

By acknowledging my negative feelings toward my father, I have become able to fully appreciate my positive feelings about him. My father was poorly educated. He was very unambitious, and I held him largely responsible for keeping us in an impoverished state. I also forgave him and began to recognize that it was not his fault, although I had thought it was.

After accepting the negative feelings, I had a

eciation of the positive ones. I have
mories about him as a sweet, happy-go-
guy. I got a lot of my good humor from
m, and the capacity to enjoy life. My father
lived in the moment. He was a genius at
that—he didn't worry about tomorrow.

The most fundamental tension of opposites,
I think, is the struggle—especially when you're
seriously ill—between wanting to live and
wishing to die.

There are some times when you want to stay
in bed and be taken care of. You don't want to
put out any energy. That feeling is nothing to
worry about. If it gets to a further extreme, you
start to feel you want to lie there and just pass
away. You may feel like giving up sometimes,
but the important thing to remember is you
don't always feel that way. When you think you
want to die, ask yourself, "Do I want it forever
or just right now?" If it's for the moment, why
not indulge the fantasy for a little while? But if

you want it forever, and you're withdrawing from life, staying in bed all the time, you are giving over to dependency and, perhaps, depression. You may need counseling.

Normally, opposite emotions alternate: one dominating now, the other dominating later. It is what dominates most of the time that determines your state of mind.

There's a joke that can be applied to our need to accept the seemingly contradictory feelings we have. A couple comes to the rabbi. The husband gives his side of the story, and the rabbi says, "You're right." Then the woman gives her side of the story, and the rabbi says, "You're right." Then the husband says, "But, Rabbi, how can we both be right? She's right, and I'm right?" The Rabbi says, "You're right."

If you find yourself fantasizing that you are no longer sick and have been restored to your previous level of functioning, stay with the fantasy as long as it gives you pleasure. But return to reality when the fantasy becomes painful or when it is otherwise necessary for you to do so.

❧

I think fantasy is very good. You should allow your imagination to roam all over the place as long as it doesn't make your reality more painful to you.

One day I was dreaming I was running, full of speed and vigor. I said, "Wow! I don't have ALS." I was ecstatic! Then I woke up.

Sometimes when I listen to music, I close my eyes and imagine myself dancing around the room. The fantasy gives me pleasure, but only for a while. If I allowed myself to dwell on it too long, it would sadden me when I opened my eyes to reality.

Come to terms with the fact that you will never again be fully physically comfortable. Enjoy the times you are comfortable enough.

❧❧❧

Acceptance is not passive—you have to work at it by continually trying to face reality rather than thinking reality is something other than what it is.

People with great faith in God or strong spiritual ties may be more accepting of what goes on here and now because they know that this is just a temporary stopping place to the next world, so to speak. If you don't have that faith, you may have to rely more on your own courage.

Acceptance is not a talent you either have or don't have. It's a learned response. My meditation teacher made a great point about the difference between a reaction and a response: You may not have control over your initial reaction to something, but you can decide what your response will be.

You don't have to be at the mercy of your emotions, and acceptance can be your first step toward empowerment. You may not be able to change your medical prognosis, but you can control the destructive emotions that can subvert your mental and physical health. For me, acceptance has been the cornerstone to my having an emotionally healthy response to my illness.

5

Reviewing the Past

*Accept the past as past, without denying it
or discarding it. Reminisce about it, but don't
live in it. Learn from it, but don't punish
yourself about it or continually regret it.
Don't get stuck in it.*

*L*iving in the moment doesn't mean reject-
ing the past. It means you react to whatever
is happening now. If you're thinking about the
past, for the moment that's where you are emotionally. Some older people or people who are
gravely ill have lots of regrets. "If only I had
done this. If only I had married that woman. If

53

only I had taken that career step." They're stuck in the past, and it is such a waste of time. Rather, look at the past and ask, "What can I learn from it? What did I learn? How does it help me right now?"

For those caring for a sick relative or friend with whom you have had a strained relationship, it is very important to come to terms with the past, for your sake as well as your loved one's. Anger and resentment don't take a holiday just because one of the parties is seriously ill. However, the caregiving relationship becomes doubly stressed if you are angry with a loved one who is sick and needs you. Relationships often are very complex. But when a loved one is seriously ill, this is not the time to rehash the past with that person. If you have not resolved conflicts prior to this health crisis, set those conflicts aside. Keep in mind that not everything needs to be resolved for you to reach a point where you are able to be an open and loving caregiver.

In terms of talking about the past, follow the ill person's initiative. Some will want to talk about the past; some will be selective about which parts they want to discuss; others may not want to talk about the past at all or may feel more comfortable talking about it to an outsider.

People are comforted by knowing that their spouse or loved one supports them in the way they want to carry on through their illness. You should gently ask questions and follow the sick person's cues. Know that the way you want to handle things may not be her way, and respect her choices. Take directives from her about what she wants and needs.

Learn to forgive yourself and to forgive others. Ask for forgiveness from others. Forgiveness can soften the heart, drain the bitterness, and dissolve your guilt.

❧☙

I think so many of us are too hard on our-selves for what we didn't accomplish or what we should have done. The first step is to forgive yourself for all the things you didn't do that you should have and all the things that you did do that you shouldn't have. Get rid of the guilt. Negative feelings don't do you much good. The way to deal with them is to forgive yourself and forgive others.

Forgiveness is a tricky term. It does not only mean that you apologize, although regretting what you did is part of it. You may want to make amends if you can, but there are some cir-cumstances where there is nothing more you can do. Even when you cannot mend fences with others, you need to tell yourself, "Yes, I did it and it would have been better if I hadn't, but now I want to forgive myself for having done that negative deed."

Forgiveness helps you come to terms with

the past. I've learned how to forgive myself, and this has helped me no longer feel deep regrets or sadness about my past.

For twenty years, I went around feeling terrible about the fact that I had treated a colleague very meanly. He was in an organization with me, and I did not want to lead a group with him. For all those years I carried around the guilt that I had been unkind to him and that it wasn't right. When I saw him again recently, I went up to him and said, "Look, I've carried this burden for twenty years. I really feel terribly apologetic for what I said and did to you, and I really want to ask your forgiveness."

He said, "Oh, it's perfectly all right. I remember the time when I was feeling dejected and low and you put your arm around me and were comforting."

I felt tears in my eyes because of the generous way he responded to me and the relief I felt.

All the work you have actively done on yourself—all the experiences you have had in your life—can be used to maintain your composure. You have these resources. Draw on them.

᙭

There's a difference between using your past and wallowing in it. Say I had an experience with a nasty person and I got nasty back, but I don't want to be that way anymore. I can use that experience to work out a different response whenever someone is not so pleasant to me. If I don't like my reaction, I can change my response.

You can review your past, benefit from your successes, and learn from your mistakes without judging yourself. This is an excellent time to do a life review, to make amends, identify and let go of regrets, come to terms with unresolved relationships, and tie up loose ends.

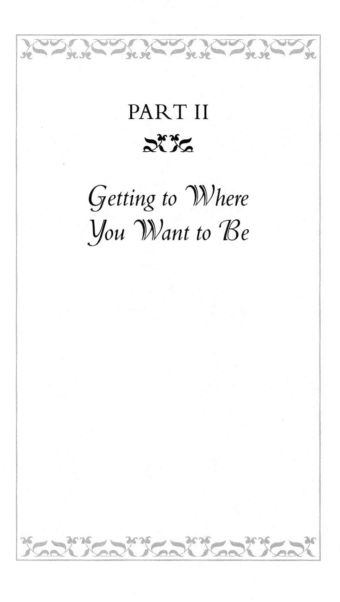

PART II

Getting to Where You Want to Be

 6

MAINTAINING AN ACTIVE
INVOLVEMENT IN LIFE

Be occupied with or focused on things and issues that are of interest, importance, and concern to you. Remain passionately involved in them.

Some people sleepwalk through life, not passionately involved in anything, but that's not the way it is for most of us. I believe the potential of passionate involvement is there in everybody. If you are feeling apathetic, take the time to assess what your interests are. What do you really care about? What have been the driving forces in your life? Who are you?

I have developed a clear image of myself, partly by identifying what's important to me. I try to see reality for what it really is, to rid myself of all the conditioning that I've been subjected to. Look beyond society's conditioned responses and effects, so you see reality for what is.

You have to be aware of what is before you can experience fully the "isness" of things in this world. What do I mean by "isness"? Think of it this way: What is the essence of a tree? What is the essence of the human being? It's really quite a mystery in some ways.

What is the essence of yourself? Who are you when you think of yourself? Are you all the roles that you play? Are you more than your roles? We used to discuss that in sociology—are you more than a role player? You're a family member, you're a worker, you're this or that, but is there something else besides all these roles?

The sociologist Erving Goffman said that

when you peel the onion, layer after layer, eventually there's nothing there. The deconstructionists say the same thing about the essence of who you are.

I don't believe it. I tend to think that we do have a core self. And that the more you know about who you are, the more actively you can be involved in the world around you.

I believe that even though each person has an individual and unique self, the self means nothing outside the context of community or meaningful contact with other people.

> *Resist the temptation to think of yourself as useless. It will only lead to depression. Find your own ways of being and feeling useful.*

❧☙

One of the great dangers when you're seriously ill is that you can begin to feel purposeless.

What are you doing in the world? Why are you here? Just to exist from day to day? If you don't have a purpose, you become depressed and start to wonder why you should bother getting up in the morning.

It's very important to set goals for yourself, even if they are very small, like cutting out some newspaper articles you've been meaning to save. Or establish more significant goals, like helping take care of your grandchild if you're able to do that. Or plan to start that book you want to read. The bigger the purpose, the more motivation you will have to really get involved in life even while you're dying.

I have multiple goals to help give my life meaning. Dealing warmly and closely and lovingly with my friends and family is a top priority. There are plenty of books I plan to read. I have my favorite pieces of music I look forward to hearing.

Don't think that just because you're sick, you can't have goals. Select your own objectives and get to work on them, no matter how slight they may appear to be. There may come a time when you can't do whatever you are trying to do. I may come to the point where all I can do is lie in bed, but until that happens, I'll continue to be as active as I can. If I reach a point where I am unable to speak or move, I still might be able to accomplish one of my purposes by being an inspiration to other people who want to be able to die with some kind of inner peace.

Don't assume that it's too late to become involved or to redirect your interests.

🖎🖎

It may be too late for you to do some things, but there are always other opportunities for you to be involved in something.

Although I had taught college for many years, I did not expect my retirement to be as active as it has been since I became ill with ALS. I started writing these aphorisms for my own benefit. It was a way to distance myself from my illness and remind myself of what I needed to do to maintain my composure throughout my illness. I wanted to get a hold on what was happening to me, and I wrote down what I was going through because that helped me objectify my experiences and be a witness to my own process.

After a while I wanted my friends to know what I was going through, so I sent some aphorisms to my friends Maury and Phyllis Stein. Maury encouraged me to share the aphorisms with other people, not just my family and friends. He said, "It could be very helpful. Not only to sick people but to lots of other people." Phyllis and Maury talked with Alan Berger on the editorial staff of the *Boston Globe* and encouraged him to have a story written about me and the aphorisms. Alan got in touch with Jack Thomas, who came and interviewed me three times before writing the article that later appeared in the *Globe*.

Richard Harris, senior producer of *Nightline,* is a former Bostonian who saw the article in the *Globe.* He showed the story to Ted Koppel, then called me and asked if I would be interested in being interviewed on *Nightline*. I agreed because I wanted to get the message out. The crew came the following day. They spent eight to ten hours filming friends, our house, and me with friends and staff who were helping me.

How did I feel about talking to ten million people? That's a whole lot more people than ever attended my lectures at Brandeis! I was pleased so many had heard what I had to say but also happy that I was being different from how I ordinarily am. Believe it or not, I'm usually a rather shy person and not very outgoing in public. Appearing on TV was a good experience for me. I was pleased to hear from approximately one hundred and fifty people who wrote to me after my *Nightline* appearances to say they had been moved or touched by what I said.

My own circumstances may be very different from yours; you may not have an opportunity to be interviewed on television or write a book, but everyone has the opportunity to be involved with people and make a contribution to others. Even a smile of encouragement to someone who is having a bad day can make you that person's inspiration.

Take in as much joy as you can whenever and however you can. You may find it in unpredictable places and situations.

❧

You can find joy in practically any situation if you are open to the experience of happiness. Even a mundane task such as washing dishes can become an occasion for pleasure if you let yourself marvel at the colors in the soapsuds or let the sight of a plate remind you of the last holiday meal you spent with family or friends. Whatever your activity, do it with care and consideration and awareness. If you focus on doing the best that you can under the circumstances, without making yourself anxious or nervous about it, you might find that what you are doing becomes a source of enjoyment and pleasure rather than just a chore.

7

RELATING TO OTHERS

*Keep your heart open for as long as you can,
as wide as you can, for others and especially
for yourself. Be generous, decent,
and welcoming.*

During the course of this illness I've made a half a dozen or more new friends, people I had not met before. I've also reestablished ties with people I had been out of touch with for years, including former students who contacted me after hearing that I was ill.

If you are lonely, it's not too late to develop new friendships or reconnect with people you've known. Even if you have not been a friendly or approachable person in the past, there is still time enough for you to change. But you're not going to become a more benevolent person just by the fact that you are dying; if you were a curmudgeon before, you'll still be one unless you make an effort to change.

Wanting to be different is just the beginning. There's no single way to go about changing the way you relate to others, but here are some suggestions. Identify what behavior you'd like to change; try to be specific. For example, if you don't want to be a curmudgeon any longer, you might set as your goal to be more cheerful or more outgoing. Then you need to identify things you can do toward accomplishing your goal. Your first step may be as simple as saying "Good morning," "please," and "thank you" more often. If your goal is to have people talk to you more often, work on being an attentive and concerned listener. If you want people to visit you more often, work on making their visits more pleasant for them.

You may feel a little uncomfortable for a while, especially if you worry that you are merely going through the motions or pretending to be what you are not. Look at it this way: What made you a curmudgeon, or whatever, was the fact that you acted like one. When you act like a kind and generous person, you eventually become one. However, don't push yourself too hard or try to change too quickly; otherwise you may become discouraged and give up. Also, don't expect others to notice or accept your changes immediately. Some people may never respond to you as you would like; others may take a while to warm up and want to associate with you.

No matter how others respond to the changes you make or how successful you are in your attempts to change, you will be a better person for having tried.

Recognize the difference between what you want and need. Your need to feel connected to other people is as vital to human survival as food, water, and shelter.

I have become more and more dependent as my disease has progressed. I am being wheeled around to get everywhere. I am fed, bathed, taken to the john. A whole host of things I did independently and took for granted as being part of my physical self are now done for me by other people. Although I am dependent, I have an independent mind, mature emotions, and I use my independence to keep my essential self going.

There are two points I want to make about how we relate to others, especially in the context of dependency. First, no one is ever fully grown up. We are so involved in our individuality (especially in the Western world) that we don't recognize that before we can be completely grown up we have to be a member of a grown-up community. Yet we don't have any grown-up communities, that is, communities or a world in which everyone takes responsibility for each other. As Jesus and other great leaders have said, "We are all brothers and sisters," rather than alienated nomads trying to do the best for ourselves.

When you're a child, you feel a sense of community in your family and on the playground. You lose that sense of community, though, when you go to school, where right away you're made to be competitive and to try to be better than someone else. You lose your sense of community in the world of business. You lose it in the world of politics, where one nation or group is pitted against another. To be fully human is to accept your interdependence as a member of a community. Then you can have a different attitude toward needing people and being needed.

The second point is that people need to be needed. Think about it. You like to be asked for your input; you want to give it. Helping someone else makes you feel like a good person. Everyone wants to feel that he or she is a good person, whether or not this is so. The need to be needed is a powerful impulse, so be aware that when you accept someone's help, you are also giving back something.

When you think about accepting help and support, take a moment to differentiate between your needs and wants. People tend to mix these up. You might say, "I need to buy a new car," but the truth is that you want the car. What you really need is to have a loving relationship with someone or to experience the world in a way you haven't done before.

When you are ill, it's very important to be able to identify your needs and wants. I may want nice food or ice cream, but I really need to be taken to the john. A need must be acted on, whereas a want is more optional. If what you want isn't available, you may be able to get by without it.

I insist on my needs being met because I feel they're essential. I used to be very reserved and undemanding, but I no longer am. I don't want to suffer, so if I need to have my helper adjust my leg because my foot is wedged against the wheel of my wheelchair, I am clear and direct in saying that I need to have my foot moved. If I want to have the thermostat adjusted because I'm too hot or too cold, I will make that request with less urgency. Buddhists have an interesting outlook on pain. They say suffering happens— and you have a right to suffer. The way out of suffering is a meditative path. According to Buddhist teaching, if you have pain, you might be able to handle it by meditating on the pain, thereby decreasing its power over you. But they're not saying you should persist with the pain if you can do something about it. At least, that's my understanding of it.

Talk openly about your illness with those who'll listen. It will help them cope with their own vulnerabilities as well as your own.

⚖

Our culture promotes very negative attitudes toward illness, as if being unwell were some sign of weakness or a personal shortcoming. People are made to feel ashamed of being sick, especially if they are seriously ill, and this can lead one to feel guilty about being ill, even to despise oneself for being ill. Sometimes family members and friends of a person who is deathly ill withdraw from the person at the very time when he or she needs love and support the most.

There is a kind of secrecy about illness, and it hurts us all. It causes a person who is sick to feel isolated and miserable. But it also makes the person's family and friends feel disconnected from their loved one. By trying to avoid talking about what is so important to them, each person feels not only fearful and guarded but alone.

I find it very important to be able to share what's going on inside me with others. I don't talk about it to everyone, but I do tell my family and friends. It's my hope that they will be responsive and supportive. Also, if they know what is actually happening to me, they won't imagine things that may be worse than they really are.

We talk about my condition as something that is continually present but that doesn't constitute our whole relationship. So we can talk about it without our becoming preoccupied with it or having it constantly be the theme upon which we relate to each other.

I am not suggesting that you stop people on the street to talk about your health problem, but do talk about it to someone. Don't keep what you are going through bottled up inside. Don't shut out other people.

After I appeared on *Nightline,* I read Eric Mink's column in the *New York Daily News,* in which he said of my segment that "Ted Koppel has used television to open a pathway into the hearts and minds of the dead." He wrote that his father had had ALS and had refused to talk about it. His father withdrew and wouldn't share any of his feelings or thoughts, so his son hadn't the slightest clue about what was going on with his father. When Mink saw me on television, he "felt as though [he] finally was hearing some of [his] father's secret thoughts."

When you open up, those who are close to you will be appreciative and helpful, and you will feel much better about yourself.

Maintain and continue a support system, individually and collectively, of people who care about you and vice versa. Do not make demands that others are not ready or willing to fulfill. You may drive them away. Accept their refusal graciously.

❧

There has to be a caregiver; you really can't manage serious or long-term illness on your own, regardless of how self-reliant you've been. It is obvious that you need someone to look after your physical needs when you are incapacitated, and that you need a surrogate or advocate to oversee your medical needs when you are no longer able to participate fully in making decisions about your care. But you may not be as aware of how crucial it is to have someone care for your social needs.

If you become ill and no longer have the strength to write letters or make lots of phone calls, your caregiver can become your lifeline. For example, your caregiver can reach out to an estranged or distant relative or friend and say, "I know he'd really like to see you. Just come." Or if you are no longer up to seeing many people, she can say to callers, "Today has been a bad day. Why don't you call again next week."

I love having my family and friends around me, but not everyone likes to have lots of visitors. Some people may prefer to spend their time almost exclusively with close family or with an old friend. Whatever is right for you, don't hesitate to let your wishes be known. If you want someone to come to visit, go ahead and ask. If someone says, "Let me know if there is anything I can do," don't let pride or humility keep you from replying, "It would be nice to talk to you from time to time. I find that very helpful." If you just can't be that forthright, ask your caregiver to tell the person that you would appreciate a call or visit.

Support systems are essential when you're in a state of disrepair. I am lucky to have a whole stream of friends coming through my house. I call them my support community, my angels, my dear friends. They come quite regularly to find out how I am, to exchange thoughts about spiritual issues, to let me know how much they care. Sometimes they bring dinner. They come to have dinner with me, to communicate about the news of the day or what's happening in their lives, to tell me about issues they're struggling with, things about which I might be able to offer help or advice.

As a matter of fact, there is a great deal of interchange, my giving to them and their giving to me. They tell me they are learning from me, that watching me is an inspiration to them. And in return I feel that they're continuing to keep me alive because there's so much energy and good feeling, love, concern, and care that comes from these friends, as well as from my family. Since I'm so restricted in my movements, they bring the world in. They bring themselves in. By their bringing the world in, I can get outside to some degree.

I am mindful of not making too many demands on people. That's because I want my friends and family to be able to maintain their normal lives as much as possible. I don't mind if

I make a demand and they say no. I try to be very sensitive to where people are coming from. Before making any demands on someone, take into consideration whether he or she has a sick parent, kids to watch, difficulties at work, marital problems, or other burdens. That person may already have a full plate, as they say.

Know that your friends and family may see you as less incapacitated than you are because they want you to be "better." They have this need because they care about you. Accept this, while trying to convey your current reality without imposing it on them.

❧

My friends, family, and helpers all have a tendency to hold the Kleenex box too far away when I ask for a tissue. They automatically keep it at a certain distance, but it is now beyond my reach because my hands are too weak. Of course, they move the box closer when I mention it, but they still haven't routinely caught up with the fact that my arms have deteriorated so much. In that little act, they're saying to me, *We still believe you're in a better place than you are now. That you're back where you were two weeks ago, four weeks ago.* I know that it's hard for them to accept the changes because it's even hard for me to remember. Sometimes I'll reach out, thinking I'll get the Kleenex, and then I can't. But it's easier for me to recognize the changes than it is for the people around me, because I'm experiencing them time and time again. They want me to be more able-bodied than I am; they want to believe I'm still capable of doing all the things they habitually saw me doing in the past. So when I tell them I can't reach the tissue, they move the box closer, but the next time they do the same thing. That's how I know that they've not fully accepted my new plateau. Each time I have to ask to have the box brought closer, I remind myself that eventually they'll catch up with my present level of dysfunction, just as I caught up with it myself.

Let others' affection, love, concern, interest, admiration, and respect be enough to keep you composed.

✄

People come with their love, their affection, and their caring, but it's not always easy to be responsive. Let me give you an example. Sometimes people tell me, "You look beautiful," or "You look luminescent, angelic." And I'm saying to myself, "Who, me? You're talking about me? I'm a sick man." But that's not right. They are sharing with me their experience of me, and I should permit myself to be open to their experience, even when it is contradictory to how I'm actually feeling. I remind myself to let all the good things come in. You can't avoid the bad things coming in physically because they're inevitable, but you can choose to accept the good things whenever they come along. These loving moments help fortify you and keep you feeling more composed and at peace.

8

BEING KIND TO YOURSELF

Be loving, compassionate, and gentle toward yourself. Befriend yourself. Do not put yourself down or criticize yourself continuously.

I think a lot of people beat up on themselves, punish themselves emotionally because they're "not good enough" or they haven't done enough. They berate themselves for not living up to their own or somebody else's expectations or for not having taken a different route in life or for not getting better grades in school or a better job.

There are many reasons you might be un-kind to yourself and continue to harass yourself. But this is just not beneficial, especially when you are ill.

When you are sick, it's easy to feel disgusted with yourself, to feel responsible for your illness, or to feel that you are being punished and, therefore, you deserve to be sick. You may think that you are no longer a worthwhile person be-cause you're sick. Once you get into that state of mind, you continue to be mean to yourself and hurt yourself in ways you may not even be aware of.

It's very important to be kind and loving to yourself. You're the only self you've got, so to speak. Befriend yourself in the same way you feel compassionate and gentle with other peo-ple. If you practice the principles of grieving, accepting, and forgiving yourself, you will be making a start in that direction.

Our whole culture derides us through fostering competitiveness in all aspects of life. If somebody wins, somebody has to lose. So you criticize yourself, you put yourself down because you haven't done better, you haven't won, you haven't been number one. But what's wrong with number two or three? We should stop evaluating ourselves in such ways that do injury to our emotional or physical state. Every time you think of something bad about yourself, think of something good. Think of something positive. Think of ways to be kinder and more nurturing toward yourself.

Being gentle to yourself is a bit like parenting yourself, showing the patience, encouragement, and kindness to yourself that you may have received from your parents as a child or given to your own children. I use my memories of my stepmother as one of my models for being kind and nurturing.

After my father remarried, we were still poor, but our lives were much richer emotionally. My stepmother had no children of her own and cherished my brother and me. My stepmother was a vital part of my life, and I loved her dearly. She was my savior, a very loving and moral person. From her, I got many of my ethical ideas: Be honest, be truthful, be kind to other people, be concerned for others. And I apply the loving principles I learned from her to how I treat myself.

Find ways to maintain your inner privacy even when your privacy is being invaded by external necessities.

When you're sick, privacy becomes a valuable commodity because it's very hard to come by. As I get more and more dysfunctional, I have to suffer more invasion of my privacy.

Since I require twenty-four-hour daily help, there is always someone nearby. My helpers are very considerate. When I want privacy, they'll leave me alone. But there are times when I would like privacy and I can't have it. Although I could feed myself when I started this book, I have now reached a point where it's not possible for me to sit and eat lunch alone. And so I have to be fed.

When I talk about privacy, I'm referring to having time to be with yourself and in communication with yourself. If other people are around, it's harder to do this. And I think we all need that time to find out where we are, what we're feeling, what we're thinking, and how we're relating to the world. So what I have to do is develop an inner space. My private space where my thoughts and emotions are. My private space for meditation and contemplation.

If you are ill, you can experience more freedom to be who you really are and want to be because you now have nothing to lose.

Although you may be old or sick, it's not too late to take stock and ask yourself if you really are the person you want to be, and if not, who you do want to be.

Martin Buber, a Jewish philosopher, wrote a poetic book of spiritual teaching called *I and Thou* in which he tried to portray an ideal type of relationship. I understood the I-Thou relationship to mean that you and I would be reciprocally related but not lose our individuality. I have carried this farther: You should find out who you were meant to be and get in touch with an inner longing or a sense of yourself in terms of what your potential is and what you could become. If you discover this, try to achieve it—whatever it is.

I'm saying you can do that even in the last year of your life. In fact, you may find it easier to make changes because you now have the freedom of having nothing to lose. So if you want to be more kindly and compassionate, start being more kindly and compassionate. If you want to be a meditative person, start meditating. What were the qualities you longed for when you were younger or when you were well? Now is the time to work on becoming the kind of person you would like to be.

 **9**

DEALING WITH YOUR MIND AND EMOTIONS

Try to compensate for the loss of control of parts of your body by increasing control over your mind and emotions.

𝕏

*P*rolonged illness can play havoc on your emotions. The key is to learn how to direct your emotions instead of allowing yourself to be led around by your fluctuating feelings.

You can't control your emotions by will-power alone or by saying that's what you want. If you have ever tried to break a habit like biting your nails, you know you don't stop by saying to yourself, "Stop biting my nails." You have come to some kind of emotional understanding as to why you're doing what you're doing and what purpose it serves. Sometimes you know that cognitively; sometimes you might know it unconsciously.

Directing your emotions involves working through on an emotional level the issues that you confront and having enough emotional space, so to speak, to handle these issues without being overwhelmed by them. By "emotional space," I mean that you're not locked into a particular way of feeling and thinking, that you can see and connect with alternatives. You can exercise considerable influence over your emotions by recognizing that you have emotional choices.

I discussed the difference between a response and a reaction in chapter 4. When something happens, we usually have a spontaneous reaction we can't control. If somebody slaps you in the face, you may get angry; if somebody speaks ill of you, you may get resentful. If somebody tells you you're a great person, you may become happy. Those are reactions. Next, you may step back and say, "I don't want to react that way." Of course, you aren't as likely to say that in positive situations as in negative ones.

You might decide you don't want to be resentful because that gives the other person a certain amount of control over you—the power to force you to be resentful. When I want to change my response to something, I work on understanding why I react as I do. I'll ask myself, "Why am I so resentful? What is the big deal about this? So he said something mean about me? It's his problem, not mine." The idea is to try to gain more control of the response you give to your emotional reaction.

I know that directing your emotions is not easy, and you may need a reminder from those around you. Let me give you a case in point. I have been receiving lots of letters and cards since people have learned I am ill. Sometimes I would get together with a small circle of family and close friends, and they would help me answer my correspondence.

One of these letters was from a couple who had been estranged from me for many years. Frankly, I did not really care for the letter, so I wasn't going to reply to it. One of my sons asked, "How about that 'compassionate heart'?"

"How about my honesty?" I replied.

He said, "How about changing your feelings about how you feel about them?"

Thanks to my son, I did change my feelings about my estranged friends, and this allowed me to work further toward an open heart.

Be a witness to yourself. Act as an observer to your own physical, emotional, social, and spiritual states.

When we are in an experience, and it's meaningful or emotionally involving, we tend to be absorbed in it. Sometimes the experience is so absorbing that we're overwhelmed: We find it impossible to stop thinking about it. When you're ill, you need to learn to be both a participant and an observer in whatever is happening to you. In my own case, I had developed this capacity over several years when I was a researcher at Chestnut Lodge Sanatorium, where I observed and analyzed patient-staff interactions for a project on mental illness. It was clear that I needed a certain detachment from the patients I was observing or I would have gone crazy myself. Gradually I developed the sense of standing outside, just watching what was happening, even though the events themselves were very, very moving emotionally. There came a time when I could almost simultaneously look at what was going on while I was experiencing it.

able to do both, either simultaneously or successively. Sometimes you can't do both at the same time. You have to wait until later, when you can go back and ask yourself: What happened there? How can I detach from it? What can I learn from it?

You can do this in a number of different ways. One way is to try to stand back as if you were another person and look at yourself through the eyes of that person. That's called "taking the role of the other." George Herbert Mead, in his book *Mind, Self, and Society* (an important text for me in graduate school), proposed that kind of role taking or empathy back in the 1930s. We feel how the other person is feeling by putting ourselves in that person's place. Let me show you how you can step back and take the role of the other in looking at yourself, as if you were another person.

I look at myself, and sometimes I see a dysfunctional person, someone in need of much help. Sometimes, I see a wise old man. But I also look at what's going on with me as if it were happening to somebody else. I'll say, "If somebody else were going through this, how would it look?" By projecting my experiences outward, I don't have to be fully identified with the subjective process of my illness.

Another way to detach or witness what is happening is to write things down. By writing it down you gain objectivity. So if I write about my ailments, my pains, and my dysfunctions, I can get outside of myself. A symptom becomes something I can analyze and think about rather than a purely subjective experience. If a moment is especially sorrowful or painful, it may be difficult to get distance from it. But by and large, I'm able to get some perspective on many of the major events related to my illness by getting some detachment from them.

Distancing also can be accomplished by

being pulled into another place. That's what meditation does—it gets your mind into another space or an alternative reality. Prayer does that for some people.

I want to make it clear that I don't suggest that you try to avoid experiencing whatever you're experiencing. If you're angry, frustrated, disgusted, resentful, despairing, whatever it is, let yourself feel it—but also know that you can detach from it. If you don't let yourself really experience what's going on, it won't be clear what you're detaching from.

Accept your doubts about your ability to achieve any change in your emotional state. But keep trying. You might be surprised.

❧

We all have doubts about trying to make changes, particularly when emotions are involved. When we have doubts, we tend to surrender to the doubt, rather than doubt the doubt.

Maybe your doubts can be altered, or maybe your uncertainties are not as strong as you think they are. I have a friend in his fifties who doubts that he can live alone. I know that he can. And I feel that I know him better in that dimension than he knows himself. I have told him that I doubt the strength of his doubts, but it's very hard for him to absorb it. Still, he has made some progress on that score because his faith in my good insights allowed him to question his uncertainties about himself.

If you keep trying to handle your emotions, you might be surprised that some things will change even though you didn't expect them to. For example, I used to get very annoyed and somewhat resentful of people whom I had expected to be more responsive and attentive toward me after I was ill. I would start to feel they were not nice people. Then I began to say to myself, "Look, they have their lives to lead, and I should be able to accept the fact that they give as much as they can or want to." When I saw things that way, I was not as resentful or annoyed. Instead, I was grateful for what they could do.

Achieving complete control of your emotions is not a realistic or advisable goal. Persistence is what counts—trying should be thought of as an exercise that strengthens you. Don't approach it in an obsessive, overanxious way, but in a calm and determined way. Tell yourself, "This is what I want to work at, and I'll try to find ways of working at it."

It might help you to consider the Jamesian principle of psychology. It was contrary to the conventional wisdom of William James's day. Prior to the turn of the century, it was believed that if you feel a certain thing, you will act in a certain way. He turned it around and said, if you act in a certain way, you might feel that way. I believe it can go either way. If you act with love and openheartedness, you might start to feel that way. The other side of it is, if you act with love toward someone, that person will probably give you love in return.

Be hopeful but not foolishly hopeful.

When you learn you have a serious illness, you naturally hope that it isn't as serious as it appears to be or as you've been told it is. You may have let your hope run away with you, and you find out your expectations are quite unrealistic. On the other hand, you don't want to feel hopeless. It would be folly to think there will be a cure for ALS in time to save me, but to hope that my ALS will reach a plateau or move slowly is realistic. I can be hopeful about continuing to be effective and useful for a while longer.

Courage is a very interesting phenomenon. I don't think I would have predicted that I would be able to handle my illness as I have. I've never been a very brave person in terms of dealing with physical pain. If I were in a torture chamber and my inquisitors wanted a confession, I probably would confess fast. When my sons were small, I'd get a little anxious if anything happened to either of them, even though it wasn't very serious.

Dealing bravely with physical pain or accidents takes one kind of courage. Facing life as it is and accepting it requires another. I think I've developed some of that kind of courage over the years, especially in this last year. I have found courage through seeking thoughtfulness, openheartedness, detachment, and other responses that make up a composed life and a calm response to illness. All of these give me a sense of inner peacefulness and help me maintain my dignity, good humor, and keep up my morale. This contributes to my feeling that I'm a good person and that I deserve to have peacefulness. I hope I can continue in this way to the end so that I will die with inner peace.

10

DEVELOPING A SPIRITUAL CONNECTION

If possible, find and develop a spiritual connection and practice that comforts you.

*E*veryone has his or her own way of dealing with life's fundamental questions. How did we get here in the first place? What's our existence all about? What is the human relationship to nature? These are very puzzling questions, and I'm trying to discover what the answers are. We could explain some of this scientifically, but I don't think that's the full picture. I think it is clear some higher power exists.

I don't know what to call it, but it's something powerful.

I was brought up in the Judaic tradition. I took it for granted that God existed, and it was the Jewish God, of course. One day when I was about sixteen and encouraged by a Hebrew school teacher, I was reading and talking to her about Freud. She said that Freud believed that God is a father substitute, and I said to myself, or maybe to her, "I've got a father. I don't need a substitute." She said that was the wrong interpretation. It was meant as a psychoanalytic interpretation, not a religious one. In any event, despite her argument I became an agnostic.

I had belonged to an Orthodox synagogue and was already beginning to feel its teachings were meaningless in the sense that one didn't get a feeling of holiness, a feeling of spirituality. People would shake themselves and mumble Hebraic words that I didn't understand. There was no connectedness to God that I could feel.

I felt it was just a ritual and discovered I didn't like to go through rituals anymore. Of course, rituals can be transformed into reality, but I didn't make that leap.

My rejection of the Jewish faith came around the time Hitler came to power in 1933. Hitler and the subsequent Holocaust made it very difficult for me to believe in God. I remember hearing Hitler shouting venom on the radio, and it would make me tremble. Later when we heard what was happening to the Jews in eastern Europe, it was hard for me to believe in an all-powerful God. If he existed, how could he let this happen? Now, much later, I find myself intrigued by Jewish mysticism and am reading about this movement that I only recently knew existed.

Find what is divine, holy, or sacred for you. Attend to it, worship it, in your own way.

About ten years ago I became dissatisfied with agnosticism. I wanted spirituality in my life, and I decided meditation sounded like a spiritual practice that suited my principles.

I've gotten a lot out of meditation, even though I'm not great at it and I don't do it every day. I meditate by sitting and watching my breath and watching from moment to moment what goes on. It's a form of meditation that has been a wonderful reinforcement for my psychological and sociological approaches to dealing with being physically ill.

My predisposition to the principles of meditation goes back many years to Kristnamurti, an Indian philosopher I met in 1949 or the early 1950s. My analyst was interested in him, and when he came to Washington, D.C., I went to hear him and was very impressed.

He was probably in his fifties. He looked very thin, quite dignified, with gray hair and stern visage.

His view was that you have to question all your presuppositions about life and living—about the nature of your relationships, your society, yourself, and what you expect and accept. The world is not a given. What we think and do are not the same as what people thought and did a hundred years ago.

Even our sense of what reality is changes over time. For example, the car as essential private property is a concept we developed. There's no law of nature that says we have to get around in cars, or that individuals should have their own cars. If everyone agrees that cars are no longer wanted, soon no one will have, make, or use a car. The automobile will be gone.

Look at how quickly and completely our concept of the world became altered when we dropped the atom bomb. Suddenly, we realized that all humanity can be wiped out in an instant if a few hundred people decide that's what they want to do with the bombs they have available. We created a different sense of the solidness of the world. When you put it that way, you can understand what Kristnamurti was driving at. He was asking us to look at the wicked ways we deal with each other, though he did not use those words. Look how cruel we are. Look how murderous you are. Look at how inhumane we are to each other. Why do we behave this way? And he was saying that each individual has to come to this realization for himself or herself—that's what the path of enlightenment is all about.

Meditation has helped me feel calm and more centered as I cope with being ill and facing death. But it is likely I would have arrived at the same state without it because I would have kept trying to find ways to have inner peace. People of all faiths have always looked to prayer for serenity and solace, which can be a great comfort especially in times of illness and death. Even with a strong spiritual grounding, you may benefit from additional help in coping with the stress of serious illness. Relaxation techniques help many people stay centered when they are distressed. Psychotherapy also can be valuable, since it is designed to help people feel related or connected to life. And there may be times when medication is needed to help you regain or maintain your emotional equilibrium.

There is no one way that works for everyone. Keep looking around until you find the path that's right for you.

Seek the answers to eternal and ultimate questions about life and death, but be prepared not to find them. Enjoy the search.

❧

When you are ill, it is the time to examine ultimate questions: the mystery of birth and death, the meaning of your existence on this planet, the destiny of the human race, the conditions that produced a harmonious universe, what it means to be fully human, the nature of the spirit and soul.

My friend Jack Seeley, who was at Brandeis with me in the late 1960s, telephones me every week from Los Angeles. In one of his calls he said he wanted to quote me something because he knew I was on this spiritual search, and he has found a place for his own spirituality. He said, "This is God talking and he's saying, 'You would not be seeking me if you had not already found me.'" That's a profound statement: The fact that you're seeking means you've already established a spiritual connection. You wouldn't be looking for something if you didn't already believe that it existed to be found. Believing is what faith is about.

Some of my friends keep asking me why I

agitate myself over the quest for spirituality. My meditation teacher said to me, "Morrie, you're already a spiritual person. You're compassionate, you're loving, you have an open heart, and you're aware of lots of things. That's a spiritual person." I say that's true, but I want a spiritual sign. I want a spiritual recognition. She said, "Maybe there are signs all over, but you're not recognizing them." Another friend said, "Isn't the fact that you are able to use your illness as a platform to help others sign enough? Was it all an accident that you got this terrible disease and made something so creative out of it? Is that not enough of a sign of some power beckoning to you, saying this is your last mission?"

Do I feel frustrated by not having the spiritual oneness experience I am seeking? No, it's something I like to contemplate, something I would like to see happen. If it did happen, I would feel it, and I haven't. Lots of people say

11

CONSIDERING DEATH

Entertain the thought and feeling that the distance between life and death may not be as great as you think.

*I*t's natural to die. When we were born we made a contract (whether we knew it or not) that we were going to die. And the fact that we make such a big hullabaloo about it and are so desperate about it shows that we don't see ourselves as part of nature. We think because we're human beings we're something separate from nature. We're not. Everything that gets born dies. So that's what I'm working on, to accept that simple but very profound idea.

My meditation teacher told me something

that blew my mind the other day. She said, "Morrie, maybe your view of life and death should be reconsidered. Maybe the distance between life and death isn't as great as you think." And I said, "You mean it's not a chasm—two mountains and that big valley between? You mean it's only a little bridge across a small river?"

I had always thought that life and death are separate states of being. It's very hard—at least I thought it was hard—to comprehend that they may be not all that separate. She said, "You're an open-minded fellow. Think about this in an alternative way. See where it gets you."

Be grateful that you have been given the time to learn how to die.

Dying is both a private act and a community act. I have a loving family and many loving friends who have been brought together by this tragic event, my illness and impending death. What we're doing is taking care of each other. I keep in touch with them, and they keep in touch with me.

They come regularly, and we talk about what's going on in the world, what's going on with us spiritually; we exchange our loving feelings. We cry with each other. We talk about how meaningful we've been to each other; we touch and hold each other.

They tell me they love to come here because they're learning a lot from me about how to be courageous when you're dying. Evidently, it is very heartening and very inspiring to them to see how I am living. Their expectations also help and inspire me.

We all know that we're dying . . . day by day we're getting closer to our death. The best way to deal with that is to live in a fully conscious, compassionate, loving way.

Many people close to dying have said the same thing, and I think there is a lot of truth to it. Don't wait until you're on your deathbed to recognize that this is the only way to live. To quote Stephen Levine, "Love is the only rational act." The Beatles said it: "Love is all you need." W. H. Auden said it: "Love each other or die." Many others, including Jesus, have said it, but we don't listen.

Why don't we listen? Our egos are always getting in the way, saying, "Me, me first—don't worry about the other guy." We have to realize that we must be responsible to and for each other. That is the most loving act we can perform.

Include one or more friends in your spiritual search. You might find the path to spiritual connection less difficult.

❧❧

Some friends and I have a group we call Death and Spirituality Group, and we struggle with the issue of how to make a spiritual connection and a spiritual orientation that fits each one of us. We're struggling with such issues as: Is there a soul? Is there an afterlife? Is there rebirth? Is there anything that goes on after you die?

I say it doesn't matter what the answers are as long as you're getting a great deal out of the process of searching. Besides, in regard to what happens after death, whatever is will be, whether you believe in it or not. What I'm trying to do in this community of friends and in general is to open up people, to touch them in their tender and compassionate places, so we can recognize our common humanity.

Even if you don't have a formal group, you can ask a family member or friend if she would like to meet regularly to talk. There's never a scarcity of material to talk about when you concentrate on spiritual matters. There are so many things that I have learned, especially in one-to-one or small group discussions where you can really speak from the heart. And when you talk intimately, whatever comes up is good material because it's not only the words that count but the sense of relatedness and empathy. We get together, and we share our thoughts and feelings—that's what this group has been about for me.

When you arrive at the point I'm at, you appreciate the stark truth of the Buddhist statement that "when you're young, everybody knows they're going to die and nobody believes it." When you're facing death, you believe it.

We're all on the same ship, and it's going to sink sooner or later. One hundred and ten years from now no one who is here now will be alive. When you look at it that way, you can see how absurd it is that we individualize ourselves with our fences and hoarded possessions, refusing to recognize our commonalities.

Learn how to live, and you'll know how to die; learn how to die, and you'll know how to live.

❧❧❧

The best preparation for living fully and well is to be prepared to die at any time, because impending death inspires clarity of purpose, a homing in on what really matters to you. When you feel that the end is near, you are more likely to pay close attention to whatever you treasure, especially relationships with loved ones.

The goals I have set for myself to help me stay composed during this illness are not unlike those most of us have aspired to since childhood: to behave with courage, dignity, generos-ity, humor, love, openheartedness, patience, and self-respect. When you are close to death, it is not easier to achieve these goals than at other stages of your life, just more urgent that you try. And the more committed you are to living an ethical life, the less you have to fear having your life come to an end.

I'd like to close with an allegory that my meditation teacher told. It's a story about a wave.

There's this little wave, a he-wave who's bobbing up and down in the ocean off the shore, having a great time. All of a sudden, he realizes he's going to crash into the shore. In this big wide ocean, he's now moving toward the shore, and he'll be annihilated. "My God, what's going to happen to me?" he says, a sour and despairing look on this face. Along comes a female wave, bobbing up and down, having a great time. And the female wave says to the male wave, "Why are you so depressed?" The male says, "You don't understand. You're going to crash into that shore, and you'll be nothing." She says, "You don't understand. You're not a wave; you're part of the ocean."

That's what I believe, too. I'm not a wave; I'm part of all humanity. I'm going to die, but I'm also going to live on. In some other form? Who knows? But I believe that I am part of a larger whole.

ML

11/04